Isaiah 26:3-4
"PERFECT PEACE V"
2541

Isaiah 26:3-4
"PERFECT PEACE V"
2541

VANESSA RAYNER

authorHOUSE®

AuthorHouse™ LLC
1663 Liberty Drive
Bloomington, IN 47403
www.authorhouse.com
Phone: 1-800-839-8640

Published by AuthorHouse   09/06/2013

ISBN: 978-1-4918-1361-4 (sc)
ISBN: 978-1-4918-1360-7 (e)

Contents

A Gift . . .

*P*resented to

_____

*F*rom

_____

*D*ate

_____

God doesn't call the qualified;
He qualified the called

Ulyer and Ambous on the sidewalk of Zion Temple
Church of God in Christ
after Sunday Service.

Theme

Isaiah 26:3-4, "Perfect Peace" is the distinct and unifying composition of this book with the subtitle 2541.

Thou wilt keep him in perfect peace, whose mind is stayed on thee: because he trusteth in thee. Trust ye in the LORD for ever: for in the LORD JEHOVAH is everlasting strength. Isaiah 26:3-4 (KJV)

You will keep him in perfect peace, Whose mind is stayed on You, Because he trusts in You. Trust in the LORD forever, For in YAH, the LORD is everlasting strength. Isaiah 26:3-4 (NKJV)

In Honor of my parents, the bible verses in this book will come from the King James Version, mostly; and a little from NKJV. They were/are from the "Old School." The only Bible they knew!

First, let me expound briefly about these two translations of the Bible. The King James Version and the New King James Version are both considered "Formal Equivalence." The Formal Equivalence or literal translation is sometimes called word-for-word translation. A translation is formally equivalent if the words are mostly matching between languages. A translation into an unrelated language is not and cannot be strictly literal.

The KJV was first published in 1611 by the Church of England. The King James Version or the Authorized Version as it is known outside of the United States was the first English translation of the Bible for about 300 years. The King James Version is the most familiar English translation. Traditionally loved and accepted by all Christians. The purpose of this translation was "to deliver God's book to God's people in a tongue, they can understand." One reason so many mature Christians keep using the old KJV is that we love its style. The KJV has a beauty of style that is seldom matched. It is an excellent study Bible, and some of the best concordances are based on the King James Version.

The NKJV is modern language update of the original KJV. The purpose was to update and modernize the original KJV, but maintain that lyrical poetry quality which is so highly regarded in the Authorized Version. The NKJV stays extremely close to the King James Bible simply replacing archaic words and phrases with more contemporary expressions. It was published in 1982. The NKJV is written on the 8th grade level while the KJV is written on the 12th.

Prayer

Father, in the Name of Jesus,
I pray that this book will help everyone who reads it,
in an unique and profound way.
Father! I pray that it will even bless those who just read
the title, only.

Father God, thanks for blessing those that help make
Your Work and Word able to go forth
in a sin—sick world.

Father, You makes it clear that You will reward those
that bless your servant.
It could be by prayer, words of encourage, buying a
book,
e-mailing or twittering others about the book,
to even given that person a cup of water.

**And if you give even a cup of cold water to
one of the least of my followers,
You will surely be rewarded.**
Matthew 10:42 NLT

Father, I give you all the Glory and Honor because You
are so Worthy.

Amen

Author's Notes

Author notes normally provide a way to add extra information to one's book that may be awkward and inappropriate to include in the text of the book itself. It provides supplemental contextual details on the aspects of the book. It can help readers understand the book content and the background details of the book better. The times and dates of researching, reading, and gathering this information are not included; mostly when I typed on it.

Friday, November 23, 2012 ~ 0558; Just woke up. I had a dream about my parents and their earthly resting place, 2541. I can't remember it all, but I woke up feeling happy. I prayed about it, was going to dismiss it; when the unction of the Holy Spirit said, "write about it." I like to say, I had a lovely Thanksgiving Feast with my in-laws, yesterday. P.S: I just finished typing Perfect Peace IV about five days ago, just need to read over it, a few more times.

Saturday, November 24, 2012 ~ 0723

Sunday, November 25, 2012 ~ 1457

Monday, November 26, 2012 ~ 0702

Tuesday, November 27, 2012 ~ 0713

Thursday, November 29, 2012 ~ 0700

Sunday, December 2, 2012 ~ 1405

Monday, December 3, 2012 ~ 0740

Thursday, December 6, 2012 ~ 0555

Friday, December 7, 2012 ~ 1000

Sunday, December 9, 2012 ~ 0855

Monday, December 10, 2012 ~ 0644

Tuesday, December 11, 2012 ~ 0635

Wednesday, December 12, 2012 ~ 0631

Saturday, December 15, 2012 ~ 0611

Sunday, December 16, 2012 ~ 0507

Tuesday, December 18, 2012 ~ 0642

Wednesday, December 19, 2012 ~ 0643

Thursday, December 20, 2012 ~ 0650

Friday, December 21, 2012 ~ 0631

Saturday, March 23, 2013 ~ 1900

Sunday, April 14, 2013 ~ 0559; 7,803 words, Father God. 2,196 more words would be nice, but never the less not my will but your will Father God, in Jesus Name. Amen.

Monday, April 15, 2013 ~ 1627

Friday, May 3, 2013 ~ 0645

Friday, May 17, 2013 ~ 1615; trying to find when my parent was married, it's hard; but I got to keep searching.

Sunday, May 19, 2013 ~ 0733

Tuesday, May 21, 2013 ~0613

Thursday, May 23, 2013 ~ 0648

Friday, May 24, 2013 ~ 1718

Sunday, May 26, 2013 ~ 0559

Monday, May 27, 2013 ~ 0627; Memorial Day

Tuesday, May 28, 2013 ~ 0649

Thursday, May 30, 2013 ~ 1533

Monday, June 3, 2013 ~ 0110; Husband's Birthday

Tuesday, June 4, 2013 ~ 0001 started back at 2308; on Charlie Shift again.

Wednesday, June 5, 2013 ~ 1207

Thursday, June 6, 2013 ~ 0132

Sunday, June 9, 2013 ~ 0745

Tuesday, June 11, 2013 ~ 1215

Saturday, June 15, 2013 ~ 0653

Sunday, June 16, 2013 ~ 2229; Happy Father Day

Sunday, June 30, 2013 ~ 2230

Monday, July 1, 2013 ~0001

Tuesday, July 2, 2013 ~0231

Monday, July 8, 2013 ~ 0000

Sunday, July 14, 2013 ~ 2229

Tuesday, July 23, 2013 ~ 2234; Earlier this evening, I was truly blessed, strengthened, and encouraged by Evangelist Claretha Simmons-Dessuaso on the telephone prayer line. It blessed my soul, gave me strength to face obstacles bravely, and encouraged me to finished proof-reading this book; something I have been asking the LORD to help me do. While I was on the prayer line, Father God places in my spirit a title for another book, "Prayer." Remember, Apostle James the brother of the LORD said, "Confess your faults one to another, and pray one for another that ye may be healed. The effectual fervent prayer of a righteous man availeth much, James 5:16; and Jesus tell his disciples, "For where two or three are gathered together in my name, there am I in the midst of them," Matthew 18:20. Glory Be To God!

Wednesday, July 24, 2013; 0001

Thursday, July 25, 2013; 0301

Sunday, July 28, 2013; 1801

Sunday, August 11, 2013; 0551~ Looks over it one more time.

Tuesday, August 21, 2013; 1709 ~ Preparing to email manuscript to AuthorHouse while listening to the Prayer Line, facilitated by Missionary Donella Pierce Chambers from California. I haven't met her, Mother Cookie, Mother Nika, Mother Bailey, Mother Grover, Pastor Kameron Kirk, Evangelist Evonne Tucker, Evangelist Yvetta Williams and others yet; but I can say without a Shadow of Doubt, I have been Blessed on this Prayer Line. You are welcome to join. Here are some of the CST times 8am, 11am, 5pm, 9pm, 11pm, etc. Just call (605) 475-4825, and then enter the Pass

Code 310312#. I have a feeling you will be BLESS, too. Hallelujah!

Tuesday, August 21, 2013; 2110 ~ Still working on manuscript. I took a short break to get on the Bible Study Line. Glory, Glory, Glory!

Preface

Isaiah 26:3-4, "Perfect Peace" ~ 2541

This book is the 5th book of a series of Isaiah 26:3-4, "Perfect Peace" collection. Father God, I give you all the glory! Praise the LORD, Saints. I thank you!

It all started from how I drew near to the LORD in my workplace by keeping my mind on Him. I related numbers, you see throughout the day, everywhere, on almost everything on Him, His word, biblical events and facts.

My desire is for you to discover the power of the Holy Spirit by numbers, words, places, people, and things related to 2541. **Remember**, the LORD Jesus PROMISED us tribulation while we were in this world.

> *These things, I have spoken unto you, that*
> *in me ye might have peace.*
> *In the world ye shall have tribulation:*
> *But be of good cheer; I have overcome the*
> *world.*
> John 16:33 KJV

However, we have been PROMISED His peace while we endure these short trials, tribulations, troubles, and tests. Perfect Peace is given only to those whose mind and heart reclines upon the LORD. God's peace is increased in us according to the knowledge the LORD gives to us from His Word.

> **Grace and peace be multiplied unto you**
> **through the knowledge of God, and of Jesus**
> **our LORD.**
> *2* Peter 1:2 KJV

It is our hope that the number 2541 wills forever means something unique, biblical and bring an unspeakable joy to your heart, when you see it, this day forward. Be Bless!

Thanks

First, I'd like to say, as a disciple of the LORD, we can rest assure that when we are seeking His plan and purpose for our lives, we will be successful, because true success lies in doing God's will; not in fame and fortune.

Thanks for your support, and may the LORD richly bless you!

Acknowledgements

I would like to express my gratitude to **ALL** of God's people (the good, not so good, bad, lazy, hard-headed, stubborn, doubters, wayward, etc.) "smile" for making this possible, by your support. Thanks & Remember, "The gifts are still in YOU!"

For the gifts and calling of God are without repentance.
Romans 11:29 KJV

For the gifts and the calling of God are irrevocable.
Romans 11:29 NKJV

Introduction

This book was prepared and written to open your mind to a "Perfect Peace" that comes only from God. I'm striving to elevate you into a "Unique and Profound" awareness of God's presence around you at all time by using the number 2541.

Quite frankly, at this moment (November 23, 2012 at 0624), I'm not sure what I will be relating 2541 to in the bible. I guess, I can go back and type on the Preface, Theme, Prayer, Introduction, Acknowledgment, Thanks and Dedication for now. I believe in my heart and feel in my spirit, that it's time to fast before the LORD.

You see, I had a dream about my deceased parents. I clearly remember seeing their tombstone number 2541. The rest of the dream I can't remember, but I know I was at my parents' earthly resting place. I was looking downward and saying in my mind how much I missed them.

I woke up feeling happy. I then prayed about it. I was asking for understanding about the dream or should I dismiss this dream. After all, Thanksgiving was yesterday, and I ate until I went to bed, especially sweets . . . . *smile* . . . . and I miss my parents, especially when the holidays roll around.

You know, the LORD can't hold you responsible for a dream, if you don't understand it. I was about to dismiss it, when the unction of the Holy Spirit said, "write about it." You don't have to go searching for answers in a book or asking others what they think. The LORD will answer dreams He gives you, if you asks.

Ask, and it shall be given you;
seek, and ye shall find;
knock, and it shall be opened unto you:
For every one who that asketh receiveth;
and he that seeketh findeth;
and to him that knocketh it shall be
opened.
Matthew 7:7-8 KJV

Be enlightened and enjoy the peace it will bring in Jesus' Name. Amen.

Dedication

I would like to dedicate this book to my parents, Reverend Ambous Lee and Ulyer Moore. "RIP" as the world would say on earth.

However, Apostle Paul explains in 2 Corinthians 5:1-10, when you are absent from the body, you are present with the LORD.

Therefore, we are always confident,
Knowing that, whilst we are at home in the
body,
We are absent from the LORD:
For we walk by faith, not by sight:
We are confident, I say,
and willing rather to be absent from the
body,
and to be present with the LORD.
2 Corinthians 5:6-8 KJV

Chapter 1

Verses 25:41

Only Three

One thousand and one hundred and eighty-nine chapters (1189) form the King James Bible. The King James Bible consists of sixty-six (66) books arranged in two parts. They are called the Old Testament and New Testament.

The Old Testament covers over 2,000 years before the birth of Christ, while the New Testament over a brief time period of about 50 years concerning Christ's birth, minister, death, burial, resurrection and the growth of the His Church. The Old Testament was constructed by more than 40 different writers, while the New Testament was written by only 8; Matthew, Mark, Luke, John, Paul, Peter, James & Jude.

The Old Testament contains 39 books with 929 chapters while the New Testament has 27 books with only 260 chapters. The 39 books of the Old Testament are divided into five sections. They are called the Pentateuch or Torah, books of History, books of Poetry & Wisdom, Major Prophets and Minor Prophets.

The Pentateuch or Torah was written by Moses during the 40 years that the children of Israel wandered in the wilderness, (1450-1410 BC). The twelve historical books of the Old Testament continue to record the history of the people of Israel under the leadership of Joshua, through the period of Judges and the reign of the kings of Israel.

The books of Ezra, Nehemiah, and Esther record the history of Israel following its period of captivity under the Babylonian rule, (1050-465 BC). The books of Poetry & Wisdom were written between 1000–300 BC. The prophetical books of the Major and Minor Prophets span Israel's history from 700-450 BC.

The Old Testament described the history of the people that God chose whom the Messiah would come through. It also includes prophecies of the coming of Jesus the Messiah. According to the New Testament the Old Testament was written for our learning, also.

For whatever things were written before
were written for our learning,
that we through the patience and comfort
of the Scripture might have hope.
Romans 15:4 NKJV

Now these things became our examples,
to the intent that we should not lust after
evil things as they also lusted.
1 Corinthians 10:6 NKJV

Now all these things happened to them as examples,
and they were written for our admonition,
upon whom the ends of the ages have come.
1 Corinthians 10:11 NKJV

After the writing of the Book of Malachi, the last book of the Old Testament, the Old Testament was closed. The LORD was silent for 400 years before the New Testament.

The "New Testament" is referred to as the "New Covenant" because it reveals a covenant made with man by God through the blood of the Son of God. The New Testament brings completed revelation from God that began with the Prophets and Moses. It also demonstrates the fulfilment of the Old Testament prophecies of Jesus.

The New Testament is of primary value because it reveals the will of God for people today and it is the standard by which we will be judged. The New Testament also contains letters written to various churches and individuals informing them of a genuine Christian conduct, behaviour and responsibilities.

The New Testament was written over a period of years following the life of Jesus of Nazareth. The exact dates, various but biblical scholars have made an educated estimates on the dates by looking at historical events reflected in the text and studying the language used by the gospel authors. The New Testament was written from 35 to 95 AD.

The 27 books of the New Testament are divided into five sections, the Gospels, the book of Acts, the Pauline Epistles, the General Epistles, and prophecy. The books of Gospels were believed to be written between 50 BC– 85 BC. The Book of Acts, a historical account of the establishment of the early Christian church was written around 62 AD. The Pauline Epistles, the Apostle Paul's letters to the early church were written between 50– 67 AD.

Out of those 66 books of the King James Bible, only 17 of those books have **25 chapters** or more. They are listed below. I pray you read the title of each book slowly, and as you are reading, make an effort to remember something about that book. If you can't, just take a moment and read at least chapter 25 of that book.

NOTE: I like to say, these books are kept small in size [5 (w) x 8 (h) x 0.29 (d)], short in pages (between 99–124 pages); so that you can keep them in your pocketbook, briefcase, backpack, desk drawer, nightstand, car, and the list goes on. You don't have to hurry through this book, or the others. You can read them over, and over, and over again. Father God keeps blessing us over, and over, and over again? I just felt the need to say that. Praise God!

Here is the list of those 17 books with at least 25 chapters.

Old Testament

The five books of Moses are also known as the Law, Torah and Pentateuch.

1. Genesis
2. Exodus
3. Leviticus
4. Numbers
5. Deuteronomy

Historical Books:

6. 1 Samuel
7. 2 Kings
8. 1 Chronicles
9. 2 Chronicles

The Books of Poetry & Wisdom:

10. Job
11. Psalm
12. Proverbs

The Books of the Major Prophets

13. Isaiah
14. Jeremiah
15. Ezekiel

New Testament
First of the four Gospel Books:
16. Matthew

Acts of the Apostles' Book:
17. Acts

When I looked a little farther, only 3 of those 17 books have a **41st verse.** They are listed below.
1. Leviticus
2. 1 Samuel
3. Matthew

The point, I'm striving to make is "**25:41**" which represents chapter 25 and verse 41. It is the name of this book along with the resting place of my earthy parents, who this book is dedicated to. The events which surround these verses will be discussed later, but for now, let's read them, out loud.

**And then shall he depart from thee, both
he and his children with him, and shall
return unto his own family, and unto the
possession of his fathers shall he return.**
Leviticus 25:41 KJV

**And she arose, and bowed herself on her
face to the earth, and said, Behold, let thine
handmaid be a servant to wash the feet of
the servants of my lord.**
1 Samuel 25:41 KJV

**Then shall he say also unto them on the
left hand Depart from me, ye cursed, into
everlasting fire, prepared for the devil and
his angels:**
Matthew 25:41 KJV

My soul says Hallelujah! Maybe, it's just me. Just those
three verses from three books of the Bible spoke to my
spirit in an AWESOME way.

Chapter 2

Leviticus 25:41

The Year of Jubilee

**And then shall he depart from thee, both he
and his children with him, and shall return
unto his own family, and unto the possession
of his fathers shall he return.**
Leviticus 25:41 KJV

**And then he s+hall depart from you—He
and his children with him—and shall return
to his own family. He shall return to the
possessions of his fathers.**
Leviticus 25:41 NKJV

The scripture verse above comes from the third book of the Bible written by Moses. It was written about 1440-1400 BC, covering events between 1445-1444 BC. It was written for the priests, Levites and the people of Israel.

Leviticus is one of the first five books of the Bible known as the "Law."

At this point may I ask you just one question? Smile . . . What are the other four books of the "Law?"

8

1. _____

2. _____

3. Leviticus with 27 chapters

4. _____

5. _____

"Answers in the back of book"

The first five books of the Old Testament in the Bible are sometimes called the Pentateuch, Greek for "five rolls" and referred to as the "Torah" in Hebrew. However, throughout the book of Leviticus the people were camped at the foot of Mt. Sinai in the desert Peninsula of Sinai. The biblical people mentioned in the book of Leviticus include Moses, his brother Aaron, Aaron's sons Nadab, Abihu, Eleazar, and Ithamar. They were the Levite priests who were responsible for ministering to the people.

I can't resist, Glory be to God! What were the sins of Aaron's sons and consequence?

1. The sins of the oldest sons: Nadab and Abihu took their censers, put hot coals and added incense in them, and offered "strange" fire to God, something God had not commanded. They died immediately when fire blazed out from God and consumed them.

Furthermore, their father and brothers were not allowed to mourn their death, Leviticus 10:1-11.

2. The sins of the youngest sons: Eleazar and Ithamar burned the goat of the sin sacrifice, instead of eating it in the sacred area. They were only questioned and rebuked for wrongdoing by Moses, Leviticus 10:12-22.

Don't this make you wonder why death for the oldest two sons and not the youngest two sons?

Answer in the back of book

The book of Leviticus gives them specific instructions to carry out. It provides the laws to governor the Israelites who had been held captive in Egypt for 400 years. Their true concept of the God they were to serve had been distorted. They had learned and started worshipping more than one god, gods of the pagan Egyptians and Greeks.

The book of Leviticus gives the Israelites a brilliant understanding of the One and Only True God, and that He desires and commands them to act and worship Him in a holy manner. The word "holy" is spoken of 93 times from 77 verses in the book of Leviticus, KJV. It is mentioned here more than any other book of the Bible.

**Speak unto all the congregation of the
children of Israel,
and say unto them,
Ye shall be holy: for I the LORD your God,
am holy.**
Leviticus 19:2 KJV

The book of Leviticus describes Moses giving procedural instructions for the Israelites' Leviticus priests. He tells them how they are to conduct offerings, ceremonies, and celebrations.

The laws in the book of Leviticus apply to their sacrificial, ceremonial and ritual practices. The book begins with the burnt offerings and concludes with redemption.

Just a friendly reminder, a **burnt offering,** signified the complete dedication of the offering that is being consumed by fire, and it ascends to God in heaven while being consumed by fire. Now, **redemption** means the purchase back, buy back, or a price paid to cancel the bondage that existed by a redeemer.

The Book of Leviticus can be divided as follows:

Chapters 1 – 7 are concerning sacrifice and the five main offerings which are burnt, grain, peace, sin and trespass. The procedures that are performed for these offerings at the altar are giving in details for the Priests.

Chapters 8 – 10, Moses describes the instructions for the Priesthood. Moses consecrates his brother Aaron and his sons as priests. They become authorized to perform the religious rituals for the people.

Chapters 11 – 15, Moses teaches the distinction between clean and unclean things. He teaches the procedures for handling things that are unclean in regards to food, diseases, animals, insects, dead bodies, birth and many others.

Chapter 16, Moses gives instruction and describes the Day of Atonement. He explains how the High Priest cleanses and prepares himself for this ceremony to meet with God. The High Priest enters into the Holy of Holies once a year and offers a sacrifice to God on behalf of the entire nation of Israel's sin.

Chapters 17 – 27 pertain to the laws that apply generally for living a holy life. These laws pertain to sexual immorality, idolatry, land laws, priestly laws, religious festivals, and celebrations, the Sabbath year and the year of Jubilee.

The truth of the matter, the entire book of Leviticus represents in many ways the person and work of our Savior, the LORD Jesus Christ. Read back over the chapter's descriptions. For example, Chapters 1-7 pertain to the offerings. The burnt offering represents Jesus' death, the grain offering represents His sustenance, the peace offering maintain His fellowship, the sin offering represents Christ making peace with God, and the trespass offering represent Christ making peace with men. Chapters 8-10 relate to instructions for Priesthood; Jesus gave instructions to his disciples and apostles. Chapters 11-15, Moses teaches the people about clean and unclean things; Jesus expound on righteous and unrighteous. Chapter 16, Moses describes the Day of Atonement and in the New Testament Jesus is the Atonement, Hebrew 13:11-15. Chapters 17-27 pertain to the laws for living a holy life; Jesus taught on the same issue.

Now the chapter, I like to expound on is the 25th chapter of Leviticus. It can be outlined as follows:

Verses 1 – 7 "The Sabbatical Year B.C. 1490"

The LORD spoke to Moses at Mount Sinai, vs. 1. The LORD tells Moses when they come into the land (Canaan) which He is about to give them; it shall have a Sabbath, vs. 2. Six years they can sow, prune, and gather crops, vs. 3. The seventh year the land shall have a Sabbath rest, and a sabbatical year, vs. 4-5. Everyone shall eat the Sabbath products of the land for food, even the cattle and animals, vs. 6-7.

Verses 8 – 22 "The Year of the Jubilee"

In the year of Jubilee everyone is to return unto his own possessions, vs. 13. You are not to oppress another to buying and selling, vs. 14. Purchases are to be evaluated every jubilee, vs. 15-17. Your promises to obedience are made, vs. 18-19; and vs. 20-22, promises related to the Sabbatical year.

Verses 23—34 "Redemption of the Land and Houses"

No inheritance must be finally alienated, vs. 23-24. No advantage is to be taken of a man's poverty by buying his land, vs. 25-28. Ordinance about the selling of a house in a walled city, vs. 29-30; in a village, vs. 31. Houses of the Levites may be redeemed at any time, vs. 32. The fields of the Levites must not be sold in the suburbs, vs. 34.

Verses 35 – 38 "Compassion towards the Poor"

No Usury (lending money with extremely high interest rates) to be taken from a poor brother, vs. 35-38.

Verses 39—55 "Oppression of Brethren Forbidden"

Suppose an Israelite was sold to an Israelite, he must not be forced to serve as a slave, vs. 39, but as a hired servant or even a sojourner (a person who stays for a short time in a place; live temporarily), till the year of jubilee, vs. 40, then he shall have liberty to depart with his family, vs. 41; because God claims all Israelites as his servants. He redeemed them from bondage in Egypt, vs. 42-43. The Israelites are allowed to have bond-men and women of the heathens bought with their money, vs. 44-46. If an Israelite become poor, and sell himself to a sojourner who has become rich, he may be redeemed by a relative, vs. 47-49. Before the day of the jubilee, he may be redeemed. If he is not redeemed, he shall go free in the jubilee, vs. 50-55.

This is how the 25th chapter of the book of Leviticus portrays Christ. The first seven verses tell us that all labors were to cease in the 7th year. The land was to rest, and man wasn't going to plough on it, or sow seeds on it. Whatsoever, the earth produced this year should be eaten and not laid up. These verses teach us to be aware of covetousness, for man's life consists not in the abundance of possessions. We are to depend on God's providence and rest in His guidance and care.

Verses 8 thru 22 in Leviticus are concerning the day of Jubilee which occurred every 50 years. Rams' horns were blown on the evening of the great Day of Atonement announcing the start of the year of Jubilee. It proclaims liberty and salvation. The liberty of every man, whether he was sold or forfeited his freedom were returned at the year of jubilee. This represents our redemption by Christ from the slavery of sin.

Verses 23 thru 34, says tell us if the land were not redeemed before the year of jubilee, it was returned to the person who sold or mortgaged it. This portrays God's free grace. It's not by any price or merit of our own, we are saved and restored to the favor of God, but by His grace and mercy.

Verses 35 thru 38 tell us the poor debtors must not be oppressed. Help the poor by giving to them according to their necessity and your ability.

Verses 39 thru 55 says if a native Israelite is sold for debt, or for a crime, he was to serve six years, and to go free on the seventh. When a man sold himself because of poverty, the masters are required to give to them what is just. At the year of jubilee, the servant will be set free, along with his family and can return to his own family.

The 41st verse rests in this passage of scriptures that symbolize redemption from the services of sin and satan, by the grace of God in Christ, who set us free. Hallelujah!

> **And then he shall depart from you—he and his children with him—and shall return to his own family. He shall return to the possession of his fathers.**
> Leviticus 25:41 NKJV

NOTE: Leviticus is written specifically for the children of Israel. It contains laws and rules for Israel to obey as they prepare to occupy the Promise Land, "Canaan." I pray you read the following scriptures, and you will find enclosed "Speak unto the children of Israel." Leviticus 1:1,2; 4:1,2; 11:1,2; 12:1,2; 15:1,2; 17:1,2; 18:1-6, 19:1,2, 20:1,2; 21:1, 23:1,2, 24:1,2, 25:1,2 and 27:1,2.

The New Testament/New Covenant went into effect when Jesus died on the Cross. Since Jesus died on the Cross, God requires no one to offer blood sacrifices because Jesus had shed His sinless blood on Calvary. The blood of Jesus satisfies all the demands of God, "by that we have been sanctified through the offering of the body of Jesus Christ once for all, Hebrews 10:10. For by one offering, He has perfected forever those who are being made sanctified, Hebrews 10:14.

However, "For whatever things were written before were written for our learning, that we through the patience and comfort of the Scriptures might have hope," Romans 15:4 and 1 Corinthians 10:11, "Now all these things happened to them as examples, and they were written for our admonition, upon whom the ends of the ages have come."

Just felt a need to clarify . . . . . LORD, I Thank YOU!

Chapter 3

1 Samuel 25:41

David, Nabal & Abigail

The ninth book of the Old Testament is called 1st Samuel. This book is commonly regarded as part of a series of historical books. The historical books are listed below.

1. Joshua
2. Judges
3. Ruth
4. 1st and 2nd Kings
5. 1st and 2nd Samuel
6. 1st and 2nd Chronicles
7. Ezra
8. Nehemiah
9. Esther

These twelve books record the history of Israel beginning with the book of Joshua. In the book of Joshua, you learned about the nation's concerns, problems, issues, and entry into the Promised Land until the time of its return from exile. These books expound and explain God's law for Israel under the guidance of the prophets.

After the book of Joshua, the historical books take us through Israel's as they move from the rule of judges to being a unified nation under kings. It also records the division of the nation and its existence as two kingdoms called Israel and Judah. It records the moral decline and deportation of each kingdom. Their years of captivity is recorded and finally the nation's return from exile. The Historical Books cover about 1,000 years of Israel's history.

The 1st book of Samuel records Samuel emerges as the last judge and the first prophet. He anoints the first two kings of Israel which were Saul and David. First Samuel can be divided into two major sections:

1. The life of Samuel in chapters 1-12
2. The life of Saul in chapters 13-31

Hopefully, to bless and enlighten you, I chose to divide 1st Samuel, a little deeper. Can I Get a Smile . . . . I pray and hope this outline generate a desire to read each chapter in its entirety, day by day. Remember, these books, "Perfect Peace" are kept short and sweet, so you don't have to rush through them, in Jesus' Name. Amen!!!

<u>Samuel Earlier Life, chapters 1—3</u>

Chapter 1: The family of Elkanah (Samuel's Father); His Wife's Vow (Hannah); the miraculous birth and consecration of Samuel.

Chapter 2: Hannah's Prayer, the Wicked Sons of Eli's the priest, Samuel's childhood ministry, prophecy against Eli's household.

Chapter 3: Samuel called by the LORD.

The Ark of the Covenant Capture by the Philistines, chapters 4—7

Chapter 4: The war with the Philistine, and capture of the Ark then the death of Eli and his sons (Hophni and Phinehas).

Chapter 5: The Ark in the hands of the Philistine.

Chapter 6: The Ark is returned to Israel.

Chapter 7: Samuel subdues the Philistines and becomes the judge of Israel.

Saul is chosen as King, chapters 8—15

Chapter 8: Samuel's son Joel and Abijah were corrupt judges; Israel demands a King, the LORD tells Samuel to heed their voice, for they have reject Him.

Chapter 9: Samuel meets Saul.

Chapter 10: Samuel anoints Saul and Saul is Proclaimed King of Israel.

Chapter 11: Saul Rescues the city of Jabesh Gilead from the Ammonites.

Chapter 12: Samuel's last Speech to Israel, farewell speech.

Chapter 13: Saul's Unlawful Sacrifice; Saul begins war with Philistines.

Chapter 14: Jonathan defeats the Philistines.

Chapter 15: Saul's Disobedience (He Spares King Agag's life and kept the best of the livestock), and the LORD rejects Saul.

<u>The Rise of David, chapters 16—31</u>
Chapter 16: Samuel anoints David as King; Distressing Spirit troubles Saul.

Chapter 17: David's Victory over Goliath.

Chapter 18: Saul becomes jealous of David; David marries his daughter Michal.

Chapter 19: Saul seeks to kill David.

Chapter 20: King Saul's son (Jonathan) loyalty to David, David flees from Saul.

Chapter 21: David's Flight to the Priest at Nob and to the King of Gath.

Chapter 22: David at the cave of Adullam, and Saul's Murder on the Priests for giving David and his men food.

Chapter 23: David saves the city of Keilah.

Chapter 24: David spares Saul's life in the Wilderness of En Gedi.

Chapter 25: The death of Samuel, David's request to Nabal for food and he refused, David and his men prepared to attack Nabal's household, Abigail took initiative to give David food, Nabal dies and David marriages Abigail.

Chapter 26: David spares Saul's life a second time.

Chapter 27: David flees to king of the Philistine (Achish) in the city of Gath, and allies with his army.

Chapter 28: Saul disguised himself and went to Endor with two of his men to consults a medium.

Chapter 29: The Philistine commanders refused to let David and his men fight with them, and King Achish sends them back to Ziklag.

Chapter 30: David and his men destroy the Amalekites because they attacked, burned Ziklag to the ground, and taken captive their wives, sons and daughters.

Chapter 31: Saul takes his life and the tragic end of his sons at Mount Gilboa, (Jonathan, Abinadab, and Malchishua).

When Saul became unworthy, God's choice turns to David. God promises David and his successors and eternal dynasty.

Note: Even though, David was anointed king while Saul lived, he didn't take the throne until Saul died by his own hands. David was thirty years old when he began to reign. Samuel anointed David when he was about 15 years old, and he didn't take the throne until he was 30 years old. David spent at least 15 years in preparation for the throne of Israel and reigned for 40 years.

Jewish tradition states that the book was written by Samuel, with additions by the prophets Gad and Nathan. Originally, the books of 1st and 2nd Samuel were a single book. The translators of the Septuagint (70) separated them, and they have been separated ever since. The events of 1st Samuel happen around 1100 BC to 1010 BC covering over 100 years of Israel's history. It covers Samuel's birth around 1100 unto the death of Saul around 1010 BC. The events of 2nd Samuel cover another 40 years beginning with the reign of David around 1010 BC to 970 BC. It ends with David building an altar on the threshing floor of Araunah the Jebusite on the summit of Mount Moriah. Later, it becomes the site of the temple built by Solomon.

Note: The word Septuagint comes from the Latin "septuaginta" meaning "seventy. Septuagint is the Greek translation of the Old Testament.

The 25th chapter of 1st Samuel can be outlined as follow.

1. The death of Samuel, vs. 1.
2. David asks a rich man named Nabal for provisions for his little army, vs. 2-9.
3. Nabal refuses the request and returns an insult to David, vs. 10-11.
4. David decides to punish Nabal, vs. 12-13.
5. Young man told Abigail, Nabal's wife what happens, vs. 14-17.
6. Abigail interceded, vs. 18-35.
7. Nabal dies, and David marries Abigail, vs. 36-44.

David marries Abigail is the event that surrounds the 41st verse of 1st Samuel. Nabal's wife, Abigail had prevented David from killing innocent people because of her husband reply to David's messenger for food. David and his army were like a wall of protection to Nabal and his men who were tending sheep in the fields.

One of the servants told Abigail of the incident. She quickly loads the donkeys with 200 loaves of bread, 2 large clay jars of wine, 5 sheep that had been slaughtered, a bushel of roasted grain, 100 clusters of raisins, and 200 handfuls of dried figs. She then told her servants, to take these items to David first and then she would catch up with them. She didn't tell her husband Nabal what she was doing.

Abigail apologizes for her husband behavior. David praised her for her good judgment. She prevented David that day from carrying out his vengeance on Nabal's household.

When Abigail went back to home, Nabal was holding a feast. He was eating and drinking, having a merry old time. The next day Abigail told him about what she had done. Nabal's heart failed him, he became paralyzed, and about ten days later he died.

Soon after, David heard of Nabal death. He sent his servants to Carmel to bring Abigail back to be his wife. The 41st verse of 1 Samuel 25 records Abigail's action and words when she was told that David had sent for her.

And she arose, and bowed herself on her face to the earth, and said, Behold, let thine handmaid be a servant to wash the feet of the servants of my lord.
1 Samuel 25:41 KJV

Then she arose, bowed her face to the earth, and said, "Here is your maid servant, a servant to wash the feet of the servants of my lord."
1 Samuel 25:41 NKJV

Chapter 4

Matthew 25:41

The Sheep and The Goats

The Gospel of Matthew has 28 chapters and is the **ONLY** book in the New Testament with a 41st verse. This verse is embedded in the parable about "The Sheep and the Goats" which gives an account of the Son of Man coming in His glory with his holy angels to judge the nations. This is the final judgment for the people in the world and the dividing of them. The people who are blessed will be on the right-hand side of God. They will be welcome by the Father and inherit the kingdom that is prepared for them. The cursed people will be casted into the eternal fire with the Devil and his angels.

The 41st verse of Matthew 25 reads, **"Then shall He say also unto them on the left hand, Depart from me, ye cursed, into everlasting fire, prepared for the devil and his angels."** KJV

This parable of the "Sheep and the Goats" is part of the Olivet Discourse. The parable of the "Sheep and the Goats" begins by saying, "When the Son of man shall come in His glory, and all the holy angels with Him, then shall he sit upon the throne of glory: and before him shall be gathered all nations: and He shall separate them one from another, as a shepherd divideth his sheep from the goats; and He shall set the sheep on his right hand, but the goats on the left, vs. 31-33.

The sheep on Jesus' right hand is blessed by God the Father and given an inheritance. "For I was hungry and you gave me something to eat, I was thirsty and you gave me something to drink, I was a stranger, and you invited me in, I needed clothes, and you clothed me, I was sick, and you looked after me, I was in prison, and you came to visit me," vs. 35-36. The King will reply, "I tell you the truth, whatever you did for one of the least of these brothers of mine, you did for me," vs. 39-40.

The goats on Jesus' left hand are cursed with eternal hell-fire, "prepared for the devil and his angels," vs. 41, because they had an opportunity to minister to the LORD, but they did nothing, vs. 42-43. They will ask, "LORD, when did we see you hungry or thirsty or a stranger or needing clothes or sick or in prison, and did not help you?" vs. 44. Jesus replies, "I tell you the truth, whatever you did not do for one of the least of these, you did not do for me," vs. 45. Jesus then ends the discourse, "They will go away to eternal punishment, but the righteous to eternal life," vs. 46.

The Olivet Discourse is the last of five discourses in the book of Matthew. Matthew 25:31-46 parable is Jesus' final official teaching before He embarks on his journey to the Cross of Calvary.

The first discourse is called the Sermon on the Mount in chapters 5-7 of Matthew. It includes the Beatitudes and the Lord's Prayer. The second discourse is found in Matthew 10. It provides instructions to the Twelve Apostles. In this discourse, Jesus tells them how to travel from city to city. He advises them not to carry any belonging and to preach only to the Israelites. He tells them to be aware of opposition, but have no fear. They would be told what to say and do when needed.

"For it is not ye that speak,
but the Spirit of your Father that speaketh in
you."
Matthew 10:20 KJV

The third discourse is located in Matthew 13:1-53. It provides several parables for the Kingdom of Heaven. The first part of this discourse, Matthew 13:1-35 takes place outside in a boat. Jesus spoke to the multitudes who had gathered to hear him. He spoke about the parables of the Sower, the Weeds, the Mustard Seed and the Yeast.

In the second part of the discourse, Jesus goes back inside the house and addresses the disciples. He speaks about the parables of the Hidden Treasure, the Pearl, and the Net. The fourth discourse is in Matthew 18 which is often called the Discourse of the Church. It includes the parable of the Lost Sheep and the Unmerciful Servant.

The fifth discourse is called the Olivet Discourse, and it is referred to as the Discourse of the End Times. This discourse also corresponds to Mark 13 and Luke 21, "The Signs of the Times and the End of the Age."

NOTE: Now, a parable is a short simple story of comparison. Jesus used parables to teach spiritual lessons and principles by means of earthly situations. A discourse is the term that describes written and spoken communications. Let's say a formal discussion on a subject.

The "Sheep and the Goats" parable reveal that man can be redeemed and saved, or man can be condemned and lost. The good works mentioned in the parable are not the cause of salvation but the effect of salvation. Goats can perform acts of kindness and charity, but their hearts are not right with God. Their actions are not for the right purpose. It should be to honor and worship God, and not for self-glory.

> **Not every one that saith unto me, Lord, Lord,**
> **shall enter into the kingdom of heaven;**
> **but he that doeth the will of my Father**
> **which is in heaven.**
> **Many will say to me in that day, Lord, Lord,**
> **have we not prophesied in thy name?**
> **And in thy name have case out devils?**
> **And in thy name done many wonderful**
> **works?**
> **And then will I profess unto them,**
> **I never knew you: depart from me, ye that**
> **work iniquity.**
> Matthew 7:21-23 KJV

This parable "Sheep and the Goats" is one of several parables of the Olivet Discourse given by Jesus Christ on the Mount of Olives. The Olivet Discourse is also called Olivet Prophecy. It is known as the "Little Apocalypse" because Jesus describes the end time. It is also found in Mark 13, Luke 21 and Matthew 24 & 25. These three gospels of the four gospels are called the Synoptic Gospels.

Just in Case: Matthew, Mark, Luke is the first three Gospels of the four. The fourth Gospel is called John. However, Matthew, Mark, Luke are referred to as the Synoptic Gospels because they include many of the same biblical events, in almost the same sequence, and in similar wording.

In the Olivet Discourse, Jesus speaks several parables. One parable is concerns a "Faithful and Wicked Servant" whose master punishes the wicked servant when he returns home, Matthew 24:45-51. Another parable is about" Ten Virgins" which encourages readiness and watchfulness, Matthew 25:1-13. There is a parable is concerning "Talents." It is the parable of three servants and their use and misuse of finances, 25:14-30. Jesus ends His discourse by telling the parable of the "Sheep and the Goats Judgment," explaining the division at the end of the tribulation, Matthew 25:31-46.

Shortly after the Olivet Discourse, Jesus was betrayed by Judas Iscariot into the hands of unbelievers. He was crucified, burial and rose again for us, sinners. Jesus Christ will one day return in glory to judge the world!

Chapter 5

National Cemetery

146 National Cemeteries

**Jesus said to him,
"I am the way, the truth, and the life.
No one comes to the Father except
through ME.**
John 14:6 NKJV

A "Cemetery" is a burial site. A specific area of ground in which the remains of deceased people are buried, traditionally below ground. The word cemetery means "sleeping place." Cemeteries are often known as and called churchyard, boneyard, graveyard, memorial park, burial ground, boot hill, city of the dead, crypt, potter's field, God's acre, resting place, etc.

However, a "National Cemetery" is a military cemetery containing the graves of U.S. soldiers, military personnel, veterans and their spouses. In July 1862, President A. Lincoln, our 16th president approved a law authorizing the establishment of the National Cemeteries. The National Cemeteries were created as a desire to honor the sacrifice made by Union Soldiers. It gave them a proper burial place. Fourteen cemeteries were established that year to bury fallen soldiers who had died in the service of the country. These National

Cemeteries were the beginning of today's National Cemetery Administration.

The early cemeteries were located on or by battlefields, hospitals, or POW camps, or sites where a large number of soldiers had died. After the Civil War, search and recovery teams visited hundreds of battlefields, searching for soldiers remains that had been buried. By 1870, the remains of nearly 300,000 Civil War dead soldiers were found, and buried in 73 "National Cemeteries."

Just a Note of Interest for YOU: The Civil began on April 12, 1861 when shots were fired by the Confederates on Fort Sumter in South Carolina. The new president in 1861, Abraham Lincoln was a known opponent of slavery. South Carolina, Mississippi, Florida, Alabama, Georgia, Louisiana and Texas perceived a threat, and called a state convention to form the Confederate States of America. Later, Virginia, Arkansas, Tennessee and North Carolina joined; a total of 11 states out of the 34 states, at that time. (Glory Be To God!!! The Next Book just drop in my spirit "Eleven," on June 9, 2013 at 09:37) Eventhough, President Lincoln stated at his inauguration on March 4, he had no plans to end slavery in those states where it already existed. He also stated he would not accept those states pulling away to create the Confederate States of America. He had hoped to resolve the national crisis without warfare. The Civil War ended when Robert E. Lee surrendered his troops to Ulysses Grant at the Appomattox court house, located in Virginia on April 9, 1865.

The National Cemetery Administration has undergone many policy changes. In 1873, Congress extended the right of burial in a national cemetery to all honorable discharged Union Veterans of the Civil War. Initially, National Cemeteries were only for Union Soldiers killed in the line of battle. In 1901, a Confederate section was established in Arlington National Cemetery, and 264 former Confederate Soldiers were reinterred there.

Arlington National Cemetery is the first national cemetery. It is located on the outskirts of the nation's capital in Arlington, Virginia. The first 14 National Cemeteries were established in 1862 in ten states which are listed below:

1. Virginia
2. Maryland
3. Illinois
4. Kentucky
5. New York
6. Kansas
7. Iowa
8. Indiana
9. Pennsylvania
10. Washington, D.C.

> "Therefore My Father love Me,
> because I lay down My life that I might
> take it again.
> No man takes it from Me, but I lay it down
> of Myself.
> I have power to lay it down, and I have
> power to take it again.
> This command I have received from My
> Father."
> John 10:17-18 NKJV

There are 146 cemeteries in the United States designation as the United States National Cemetery. Today, more than 3 million Americans have been laid to rest in the U.S. National Cemeteries. On May 30, 1929, President Herbert Hoover, our 31st President conducted the first national Memorial Day Ceremony in Arlington National Cemetery.

Memphis National Cemetery is located at 3568 Townes Avenue, Memphis, County, Tennessee. It was originally named Mississippi River National Cemetery until 1869. It encompasses 44.2 acres and has over 40,000 interments that span over 125 years, from the Civil War to 1992, when the cemetery closed to new burials.

Memphis National Cemetery has the second-largest "Unknown Interments." This large number of unknown interment is attributed to the long interval between battlefield burial and movement of interments to the Memphis National Cemetery. Oftentimes, the wooden cross markers that identified the original burials of soldiers have deteriorated to the point where they were no longer legible because of natural. Soldiers at that time were not required to wear personal identification tags.

Memphis National Cemetery is the burial place of the victims of the tragic explosion of the USS Sultana. On April 26, 1865, the steamboat Sultana with Union soldiers who had recently been liberated from Confederate POW Camps exploded on the Mississippi River several miles north of Memphis. Also, several battlefield cemeteries have been transferred there. In 1867, about 250 bodies of both Confederate and Union soldiers from the causalities of the Battle of Fort Pillow were moved there. Twenty-six soldiers of the 96th Ohio Volunteer Infantry are burial in Memphis National Cemetery. However, a monument honoring the 96th Ohio Infantry is located at the Vicksburg Military Park in Vicksburg, Mississippi.

Another interment is Private James H. Robinson. He is a recipient of the nation's highest military decoration Medal of Honor. He enlisted at the age of 18 in the 3rd Michigan Volunteer Cavalry Regiment, as a Private in Company B. On January 27, 1864 at Brownville, Arkansas, he performed an act of bravery. He single-handedly defended himself against a party of seven enemy guerrillas and killing their leader. He was later killed during the war, and his remains were buried in the Memphis National Cemetery. His gravesite in

Section H, Grave 4131 and it is marked with a "Medal of Honor" marker.

Other notable Soldiers:

1. Winfield S. Cunningham (February 16, 1900—March 3, 1986) was a United States Navy Admiral. He was awarded the Navy Cross for his leadership at Wake Island attacked by the Japanese on December 8, 1941.

2. George W. Grider (October 1, 1912—March 20, 1991) was a United States World War II Naval Officer, an attorney, and a Democratic U.S. Representative from Tennessee from 1965 to 1967.

3. Isaac Pearson (March 1, 1917 to March 17, 1985) was a Captain in US Marine Corps WWII, a Major League Baseball Player for the Philadelphia Phillies (1938 – 1942), and Chicago White Sox in 1948.

Greater love hath no man than this,
that a man lay down his life for his friends.
John 15:13 KJV

In Section M at gravesite 2541, you will find the resting place of Ambous L. Moore, PVT, WWII and his wife Ulyer. They are surrounded by the following Soldiers:

1. Howard A. Chambliss Jr., SCI, US Navy, WWII and his wife Faye.

2. William H. Johnson, PFC US Army, WWII.

3. David M. Barcy, SA, US Navy, Vietnam.

4. Eva L. McCloskey, Tec 5, USA Army, WWII and her husband Raymond.

5. Charles Brigance, CPL, US Army, Korea.

I only know one friend of the family that is laid to rest there, Miles Simmons, Jr., SD3 US Navy, Vietnam (9/24/45 – 07/12/81); Section M, Site 1496.

I like to give a "Special Thanks" to Eddie Lee Smith (March 4, 1934—December 4, 1968) who was a CPL US Army, Korea. His gravesite 2921 is on the front row that faces the pavement road; I drive down at the cemetery. It let me know, I'm at the right spot, and helps me find my parents resting place. They are resting six rows behind him.

**For the LORD Himself will descend from
heaven with a shout,
with the voice of an archangel, and with the
trumpet of God.
And the dead in Christ will rise first.**
1 Thessalonians 4:16 NKJV

Useful Definitions

CPL stands for Corporal in the Military.

PFC stands for Private First Class.

Tec 5 stands for Technician 5th grade. It is a special rank above a Corporal.

SCI stands for 1) Sensitive Compartmented Information or 2) Source Code Indicator

SA stands for 1) Staff Officer or 2) Secretary of the Army

SD3 stands for Steward 3rd Class

Ambous in Army Uniform, 1943

Chapter 6

Ambous and Ulyer

Parents

EARTHYPARENTS....

Everyone has them whether they are evil or good, just or unjust, righteous or unrighteous.

> **That ye may be the children of your Father**
> **which is in heaven:**
> **for He maketh His sun to rise on the evil**
> **and on the good,**
> **and sendth rain on the just and on the**
> **unjust.**
> Matthew 5:45 KJV

Don't really know where to start. I guess first, I need to thank the LORD for them. I didn't appreciate, nor understand my Dad rigid rules, harsh whipping, and seven days a week Bible upbringing; but now I understand and appreciate it.

Just between you and me, I told the other kids in church, "If I ever got grown, I was never going back to church." Oh, how foolish I was!

When I was a child,
I spoke as a child, I understood as a child, I
thought as a child;
but when I became a man, I put away
childish things.
1 Corinthians 13:11 NKJV

It's sad to say, I did just that when my Dad died on July 5, 1977. I was 16 year old when he passed on to Glory. I thank God for His mercy and His grace!!!

Note: On the tombstone it states July 6, 1977 as the day of death, it's wrong, but it's ok; not that important to me. My mom passed on September 6, 1983 on my dad birthday.

My dad had a heart attack working on his Chevrolet Impala. He was trying to replace the tail pipe in the car shed. My niece (Dee Dee) and nephew (Granville, Jr.) were here for the summer from Little Rock, Arkansas. I was working a summer job, and I called home to see could dad pick me up, but mom told me he was working on his car. She sent Granville Jr. to see how long it would be before he finished, but I told my mom I would catch the bus and hung up the phone before Granville Jr. returned. He was about 3 years old. He came back to the house, and said, "Granddaddy won't talk to me." My mom then briskly walked to the car shed to check on him, and found him having a seizure. She stated, she started howling for help, and the neighbors came from everywhere, and shortly after, an ambulance arrived. Once at the hospital he was pronounced DOA.

When I got off the bus my girlfriend, Lisa Lott was standing outside her parents' house waiting on me. She told me that the ambulance took my dad to the hospital. A few hours later, I was told by my mom, "he didn't make it this time."

It was 6 years, 2 months, and 1 day later mom died on dad' birthday. I had recently bought my first house, three streets over. I was sleeping when my girlfriend, Vanessa Fields drove over my house. Once she got out of her truck she started banging on my front door like a police. When I came to the door, she told me something just happen to my mom. I quickly put on my clothes and shoes, as I hopped in the back of her truck, and she drove me there.

The paramedics were intensely working on my mom in her bedroom. I observed them performing CPR, place an IV in her arm, place her on a stretcher, and shortly after rolled her into Ambulance 4. I thought she was still alive, I saw the cardiac heart monitoring machine signal moving up and down on the screen.

My father worked for Ivers & Pond Piano Company until his doctor placed him on a medical retirement. My mom was a house wife, and when we stayed in the Binghampton Housing Projects, she sold candy. I remember, her favorite television shows as being

Wheel of Fortune, Young and the Restless (where my first name "Vanessa" came from), The Three Stooges, Dark Shadows, Rifleman, Brady Bunch, Good Times, Gunsmoke, Beverly Hillbillies, I Love Lucy, All in the Family, and The Late Night Show with Johnny Carson (my bedtime).

Now, the television ministries, I remember watching with my parents, especially my mom were Billy Graham, Jimmy Swaggart, Jim and Tammy Bakker. My mom favorite Bible verse is Proverbs 3:5-6.

Trust in the LORD with all thine heart;
and lean not unto thine own
understanding.
In all thy ways acknowledge him, and he
shall direct thy paths.
Proverbs 3:5-6 KJV

I only remember my father watching The Jack LaLanne Show, faithfully. I remember, my dad doing his push-ups with me sitting on his back, LOL. My dad studied the word of God, attended church services throughout the week, and all day Sunday Services, much more than he watched television. In between working, studying and church, he sold Stuart Mcguire Shoes. He was also a Mason.

I can remember many nights he would be at the dining room table studying when I went to bed. He would wake me up some nights, just to pronounce a word for him in the Bible. He always stresses how important an education is. He had to chop cotton, sow seeds, pull weeds, milk the cows, feed the chicken, slop the pigs, and care for his siblings when he was a child, and didn't attend school much.

My parents were a member of Zion Temple Church of God in Christ in Memphis, Tennessee. Elder Clarence Randle was the Pastor at that time. Dad was one of his Elders until God called him home.

NOTE: I know it has been a while, but it would be nice to have a copy of his sermons. They were recorded on cassette tapes. If you happen to have one of those old messages, please email me at perfectpeaceauthor@ gmail.com. It would be appreciated! Thanks and May Father God Bless You Real Good!

"I Need Thee Every Day and Every Hour," "His Eyes are on the Sparrow," "Precious Lord," "By and By When the Morning Come" and "I Going Up Yonder to be with my LORD" are songs, I remember him sing in church and around the house; the most.

My father was born to Maggie and Andrew Lee Moore on September 6, 1924 in Crawford, Mississippi. My father had 2 brothers (Sam & Buddy) and 4 sisters (Willie Lue, Luelia, Dilicie Mae & Juanita) by his mother, Maggie. His mom later marriage Robert Alexander, and they had one son. His name was Robert Jr., but we called him Buddy.

His father, Andrew Moore later remarriage and had more children, (Ella Rae, Mary, Leatha, William & Arthur). I remember as a little girl, every time we went to Mississippi, he would visit them and preach "heaven or hell."

My mom was born in Starkville, Mississippi about 24 miles from Crawford. She was born to Virgie Lee and Adolphus Mobley on July 19, 1925. She was the oldest, also. My mom sisters and brothers are named Thelma, Lorene, Annie, Cora Mae, Lessie Mae, Frank, Jerome, Felix, Adolphus, Clarence and Andrew.

My father and mother were marriage around September 1943. They had 1 son, (AD) and 3 daughters (Easter, Vanessa, "Gail" by family and close friends, and Regina also called "Gina").

I discovered some interesting data about the surname "Moore." It is the 9th popular name in the U.S according to the U.S. Census and Social Security Death Index. It has a wide range of spellings including, More, Mores, Moores, Moors from British, and Muir in Scotland. The main definition for the surname "Moore" is from Middle English "Mor" meaning "open land." However, the Latin word relates to a native of northwestern Africa, but in medieval England the word came to be used informally as a nickname for any "swarthy or dark-skinned person."

The first recorded spelling of the family name is shown to be William de More is the in the Domesday Book of Suffolk, dated 1086. However, the earliest settler in the New World was Leonard Moore, who is recorded as living at Elizabeth Cittee, Virginia in 1624, having arrived on the ship called Bona Nova in 1619.

Surnames are often referred to as a last name or family name which has been passed down from generation to generation. A surname is typically inherited from the paternal father's line. The average lifespan of a "Moore" is age 71.

**The days of our years are threescore years
and ten:
and if by reason of strength they be
fourscore years,
yet is their strength labour and sorrow;
for it is soon cut off, and we fly away**.
Psalm 90:10 KJV

**The days of our lives are seventy years;
And if by reason of strength they are
eighty years,
Yet their boast is only labor and sorrow;
for it is soon cut off, and we fly away.**
Psalm 90:10 NKJV

Sweet Note: I attended this corner church across the street from me, the first time on Sunday, June 16, 2013. I was Bless! It was just 5 of us and Pastor Shirley Hunter.

I was sitting there enjoying myself, I observed at the bottom of the pulpit a huge grayish stone tablet with the 10 Commandments engraved on it. Guess what the 5th Commandment read!

"Honor your father and your mother"

If you remember, I dedicated this book in Honor of my Parents. What a way to end this chapter, Father God! You know how to make me smile.

Ambous to the left, then Ulyer and Vanessa (me)
my baby sister (Regina) is standing up.
We had recently moved to the upscale area called
Midtown.

Author's Closing Remarks

These three verses from the Bible were truly a blessing to me:

1. Leviticus 25:41
2. 1 Samuel 25:41
3. Matthew 25:41

I enjoyed studying each one. The book of Matthew is the only book in the New Testament with a 25th chapter, 41st verse. If I may, I would like to expound on that message, briefly.

In life, we often say "Goodbye" for several reasons. These goodbyes can be to a friend, co-worker, family, love ones, associates and others. Some goodbyes are said as we exit a person presence for a moment. We also have those sad goodbyes caused by death. I have learned through the years that death has no respect of persons. It claims the old, the young, the middle aged, and babies. It knocks on the poor man door as well as the rich man door, and those who are in between are not exempt, either. The Bible tells us that death is appointed to man, then after this the judgment. We too will say goodbye because of death, if the LORD Jesus doesn't return first.

Throughout the Bible, we see people saying goodbye for various reasons. We read about simple goodbyes, happy goodbyes, sad goodbyes and just goodbyes. Abraham had to say goodbye to Sarah, his wife because death took her away, Genesis 23. Rebekah had to say goodbye to her family when she went away to marriage Isaac, Abraham son, Genesis 24. Jacob tells his twelve sons goodbye after he blesses them, Genesis 49.

The children of Israel tell Egypt goodbye, after being freed from 400 years of slavery, Exodus 12. Soon after, Moses expresses his final goodbye to Israel before they set foot in the "Promised Land," Deuteronomy 34. Naomi kissed both her daughters-in-law before she said goodbye to them, but Ruth refused to leave her, Ruth 1. David bowed three times to Jonathan in tears as they embraced each other and said goodbye, 1 Samuel 20.

Jesus tells His disciples goodbye in Acts 1 before he was taken into a cloud, but they were reminded He will return from heaven in the same way. Jesus follower Stephen told his killers goodbye while being stoned to death, and he asked the LORD not to hold this sin against them, Acts 7. The Apostle Paul told the Elders of Ephesus goodbye in Acts 20. Paul went to the city of Troas to preach. He discovered that Titus hadn't arrived yet, he said goodbye to the city, and went to Macedonia to look for him, 2 Corinthians 2.

The "Last Goodbye" will be announced by God. After every life is judged, God will announce the sentence to each person. The lost will hear God's External Goodbye. Now, let us read this verse, again, "then shall he say also unto them on the left hand, depart from me, ye cursed, into everlasting fire, prepared for the devil and his angels," Matthew 25:41.

**"And whosoever was not found written in
the book of life
was cast into the lake of fire."**
Revelation 20:15 KJV

What must I do in order not to hear God's External Goodbye?
Glad you asked! Smile

Hear the Word
So then faith comes by hearing, and hearing by the word of God.
Romans 10:17 NKJV

Believe
He who believes and is baptized will be saved; but he who does not believe will be condemned. Mark 16:16 NKJV

Repent
I tell you, no; but unless you repent you will all likewise perish. Luke 13:5 NKJV

Confess
That if you confess with your mouth the LORD Jesus and believe in your heart that God has raised Him from the dead, you will be saved. Romans 10:9 NKJV

Baptized

Then Peter said to them, "Repent, and let every one of you be baptized in the name of Jesus Christ for the remission of sins; and you shall receive the gift of the Holy Spirit." Acts 2:38 NKJV

Be Faithful Until Death

Do not fear any of those things which you are about to suffer. Indeed, the devil is about to throw some of you into prison, that you may be tested, and you will have tribulation ten days. Be faithful until death, and I will give you the crown of life. Revelation 2:10 NKJV

May the Grace of Our LORD and Saviour Jesus Christ and the Sweet Communion of the Holy Spirit, Rest, Rule, and Abide with Us All Now and Forevermore. Amen.

Pray for the Ministry . . .

Dr. Vanessa

References

Chapter 1

1. Wikipedia, The Free Encyclopedia: http://en.wikipedia.og/wiki/Chapters-and-verses-of-the-Bible

Chapter 2

1. Leviticus: http://biblesummary.org/leviticus/1.htm
2. Leviticus: http://christnotes.org/commentary.php?com

Chapter 3

1. Wikipedia, The Free Encyclopedia: Books of Samuel: http://en.wikipedia.org/wiki/Books_of_Samuel

Chapter 4

1. The Parable of the Sheep and Goats: http://www.gotquestions.org/parable-sheep-goats.html
2. Five Discourses of Matthew http://en.wikipedia.org/wiki/Five_Discourses_of_Matthew

Chapter 5

1. United States National Cemetery: http://en.wikipedia.org/wiki/United_States_National_Cemetery
2. Department of Veterans Affairs National Cemetery Administration http://www.cem.va.gov/CEM/pdf/IS1_Jan_2011.pdf
3. Ninety Six Ohio Volunteer Infantry Cemeteries http://freepages.military.rootsweb.ancestry.com/~firstmsmcavalry/ohioinfantry/cemetaries.htm

Chapter 6

1. Easter Broadway (Sister)
2. Georgia Brooks (Cousin)
3. AD Moore (Brother)
4. Ancestry: http://search.ancestry.com

Answers:

Chapter 2

1. Genesis   (50)
2. Exodus   (40)
3. Leviticus   (27)
4. Numbers   (36)
5. Deuteronomy   (34)

God knew Aaron's heart. Aaron obeyed the "Spirit of the Law" but not the letter. Moses (or man) sometimes looks at the outward action, but God looks on the heart and your true intentions.

Aaron replied to Moses,
"Today they sacrificed their sin offering
and their burnt offering before the LORD,
but such things as this have happened to
me.
Would the LORD been pleased if I had
eaten the sin offering today?"
When Moses heard this, he was satisfied.
Leviticus 10:19-20 NKJV

Other books by the author:

From the Pew to the Pulpit

Isaiah 26:3-4 "Perfect Peace"

Isaiah 26:3-4 "Perfect Peace" The Last Single Digit

Isaiah 26:3-4 "Perfect Peace III" Silver and Gold

Isaiah 26:3-4 "Perfect Peace IV" Twelve the Kingdom Number

About the Author

I was born Vanessa Gail Moore in Memphis, Tennessee to Reverend Ambous and Ulyer Moore at John Gaston Hospital about 2:48 am in 1961. I'm the 3rd child of four and the 2nd daughter of three. There is a sixteen and seventeen age difference between my oldest sister and only brother. All my childhood was spent in church (Zion Temple Church of God in Christ) where my dad was one of the Reverend. Part of my childhood was spent in Binghampton at 3072 McAdoo Street which was a low-income housing project which have been torn down, and turned into single family homes.

I was about 9 years old when dad, mom, baby sister, and I moved over the viaduct to the edge of the upscale area called Midtown on Merton Street. I wrote my first story at the age of 12. It' short, silly and have two titles "The Lady Who out Ran the Fastest Car" and "How Women Got into Sports like Men." I still have the original typed manuscript.

The first college, I attended and graduated from was Shelby State Community College in 1984. I also graduated from State Technical Institute, William R. Moore College of Technical, The School of the Prophets, and finally Jacksonville Theological Seminary. On May 27, 2007, I received a Doctor of Ministry degree. I received my Ministry License on December 4, 2006, then on April 9, 2007, I received my Certificate of Ordination publicly been set apart for the work of "The Gospel."

My first book "From the Pew to the Pulpit" was published in August 2007. Since then I started a series of "Perfect Peace Books." The 1st, 2nd, 3rd book of this series is published under "Vanessa Buckhalter."